AI AUTHOR'S ADVANTAGE
WRITING YOUR WAY TO SEVEN FIGURES

AI INTEGRATION WORKBOOK FOR AUTHORS

JAMIE CULICAN

MELLE MELKUMIAN

DRAGON REALM PRESS

Copyright © 2024 AI4CES

All rights reserved. No part of this book may be reproduced or used in any manner without written permission from the authors, except in the case of brief quotations embodied in critical articles or reviews. For permissions inquiries, please contact info@ai4aauthors.com.

Published by Dragon Realm Press

Cape May Court House, New Jersey, USA

www.dragonrealmpress.com

AI-Enabled Technology was utilized in collaboration when creating this series.

Printed in the USA

CONTENTS

Introduction	v
Chapter 1 *My Journey to the AI Revolution*	1
Chapter 2 *Understanding AI – A Writer's Primer*	11
Chapter 3 *The Author's Mindset for Success*	19
Chapter 4 *Identifying AI Opportunities for Authors*	27
Chapter 5 *AI-Driven Strategies for Authorial Earnings*	35
Chapter 6 *Practical AI Tools for Authors*	43
Chapter 7 *Ethical Writing in the Age of AI*	51
Chapter 8 *Overcoming Writing and AI Challenges*	59
Chapter 9 *The Complete AI Author's Toolkit*	67
Chapter 10 *Crafting Your AI-Enhanced Writing Strategy*	75
Epilogue	83
FAQs *Reassurance in Answering Common Concerns and Queries*	89
Jamie Culican	93
Melle Melkumian	95
AI4CES	97

INTRODUCTION
A NEW ERA FOR AUTHORS: EMBRACING AI FOR CREATIVE AND FINANCIAL SUCCESS

In the ever-evolving landscape of writing and publishing, standing at the forefront of change has been both a challenge and a privilege. When I began my journey as a writer, little did I know that it would lead me to the crossroads of literature and cutting-edge technology. Today, as I share my experiences and insights through "AI Author's Advantage: Writing Your Way to Seven Figures," my goal is to illuminate a path for my fellow authors into a future enriched by artificial intelligence.

My story is one of transformation — from penning a middle-grade fantasy book for my daughter to becoming a USA Today Bestselling Author and establishing a thriving publishing company. This journey was marked by a series of leaps into the unknown, each driven by a passion for storytelling and an unwavering belief in innovation. The decision to venture into the world of AI was one such leap, and it has reshaped not only my approach to writing but also my vision of what it means to be an author in the digital age.

AI, often perceived as a realm of cold algorithms and impersonal machines, is, in reality, a wellspring of untapped potential for writers. This technology, when harnessed with skill and creativity, can amplify our abilities, open new avenues for income, and deepen our connection with readers. In this book, I aim to demystify AI for authors of all genres and backgrounds, showing how it can be a powerful tool in your creative arsenal.

The journey into AI is not without its challenges, but it is rich with opportunities. Whether it's enhancing your writing process, tailoring marketing strategies, or exploring new platforms for storytelling, AI can be your ally in achieving not just artistic fulfillment but also financial success. My mission is to guide you through this journey, sharing the lessons I've learned and the strategies that have propelled me forward.

As you turn each page of this book, consider it an invitation to expand your horizons. Integrating AI with writing isn't merely following a trend; it's actively participating in a significant shift in our creative process. This journey we're about to undertake is about unlocking new possibilities, pushing the limits of what we can achieve as writers and entrepreneurs. Together, let's explore how AI can not only enhance our storytelling but also open up unprecedented opportunities for our professional growth.

To a future where technology doesn't overshadow our creativity but instead, amplifies it, making our narratives richer and our professional aspirations more attainable.

Jamie Culican
Author, Publisher, AI Innovator

CHAPTER 1
MY JOURNEY TO THE AI REVOLUTION

EARLY DAYS: EMBRACE BEGINNINGS WITH OPTIMISM AND CREATIVITY

The journey of a thousand miles, as the saying goes, begins with a single step. For me, that step was more of a leap – one taken with a blend of unbridled optimism and a dash of naivety. It all started with a simple, yet heartfelt goal: to create a story for my daughter. This wasn't just about writing a book; it was about crafting a world, a narrative that would ignite the spark of imagination and wonder in her eyes.

In these early days, I was blissfully unaware of the norms and nuances of the publishing world. My focus was solely on the joy of creation, on the art of storytelling. This period was marked by an innocence and purity of purpose that I believe is the true essence of creativity. It's this spirit that I encourage every writer to embrace – the courage to create without constraints, to write stories that resonate with you before anyone else.

As you embark on your writing journey, remember that every great author once stood where you are now. They too grappled with doubts, wrestled with ideas, and navigated the labyrinth of their imagination. The early days are not just about laying the groundwork for your career; they are about discovering your voice, your style, and what you truly wish to say to the world.

Let your initial forays into writing be guided by a sense of exploration. Experiment with genres, play with ideas, and don't be afraid to break the rules. This is the time to be bold, to push boundaries, and to find out what makes your writing uniquely yours. It's also a time to be kind to yourself, understanding that every mistake is a lesson and every challenge a stepping stone to growth.

In these early stages, let optimism be your compass and creativity your map. Trust in your vision and your ability to bring it to life. The path may not always be clear, and the destination might seem distant, but every word you write, every story you craft, is a step forward in your journey as an author.

So, take that step with confidence. Embrace your beginnings with all the enthusiasm and creativity you possess. This is where your story begins. This is where you start to weave your dreams into reality.

SCALING UP: CELEBRATE GROWTH AND THE SURPRISES OF THE WRITING JOURNEY

The transition from the early stages of writing to scaling up your efforts is a pivotal moment in any author's career. It's a phase characterized by growth, learning, and sometimes, unexpected turns that can lead you to new and exciting paths. For me, this was the period when writing shifted from a personal passion to a potential career – a change both exhilarating and daunting.

As you begin to scale up, it's crucial to celebrate every milestone, no matter how small. Each completed manuscript, every reader's feedback, and every new idea is a testament to your evolving journey. This is the time when you're laying the foundation for your future as an author, and every brick you lay is worth acknowledging.

Embrace the surprises that come with this growth. You may find your writing taking you in directions you never anticipated. Perhaps a character takes on a life of their own, leading your story down an unforeseen path. Or, you might discover a love for a genre you hadn't considered before. These surprises are not just part of the journey; they are what make the journey rich and rewarding.

Scaling up also means facing new challenges – whether it's dealing with writer's block, navigating the world of publishing, or learning how to market your books. Approach these challenges not as obstacles, but as opportunities to learn and grow. Every challenge overcome is a step towards becoming a more skilled and resilient author.

Remember, growth is not always a straight line. There will be ups and downs, successes and setbacks. What matters is your ability to persevere, to continue learning, and to adapt. The writing journey is as much about personal growth as it is about professional achievement.

As you scale up, stay connected to your reasons for writing. Amidst the hustle of meeting deadlines and promoting your work, don't lose sight of the joy and fulfillment that writing brings. Your passion is the fuel that will keep you going through thick and thin.

In this phase of your career, allow yourself to dream bigger, aim higher, and explore further. Celebrate each step forward, learn from every detour, and remain open to the endless possibilities that writing brings. This is your journey, and every twist and turn is a part of your unique story.

INTERNATIONAL ACCLAIM: RECOGNIZE YOUR POTENTIAL FOR GLOBAL IMPACT

Reaching a point where your work gains international acclaim is a remarkable milestone, one that signifies not just personal success, but the broader, resonating impact of your stories across different cultures and borders. It's a moment that underscores the universal power of storytelling and the potential your words have to connect with people globally.

CHAPTER 1

As you venture into the realm of international recognition, it's important to pause and acknowledge the significance of this achievement. This is where your stories, born from individual experiences and imagination, cross seas and transcend cultural barriers, resonating with readers you may never meet but who find something in your work that speaks to them.

International acclaim brings with it a newfound awareness of the diverse audience your writing serves. It encourages you to consider the varied perspectives and backgrounds of your readers, enriching your storytelling and broadening your literary horizons. This is an opportunity to learn, to grow as a writer and as a person, appreciating the vast and varied tapestry of human experience.

This stage of your career is also a testament to the power of your voice. It serves as a reminder that what you write can have far-reaching effects, influencing thoughts, evoking emotions, and sometimes even inspiring change. With this recognition comes a responsibility to wield your words thoughtfully, understanding the impact they can have.

Embrace the opportunities that come with international acclaim. Whether it's translations of your work, international book tours, or collaborations with authors and publishers from around the world, each experience broadens your understanding and appreciation of the global literary community.

However, as you navigate this phase, it's crucial to stay

true to your authentic self. The core of what makes your writing special – your unique voice and perspective – is what brought you to this stage. Continue to write from a place of authenticity, and let your genuine voice be the guide that connects you with readers worldwide.

Finally, let this international success be a source of inspiration, not just for yourself, but for other aspiring authors who dream of making a global impact. Share your journey, mentor others, and be an advocate for the unifying power of literature. Your story is now a part of the larger narrative of authors who have bridged worlds through the power of their words.

KEY LESSONS: BELIEVE IN YOUR ABILITY TO ADAPT AND THRIVE

In the journey to becoming a successful author, reaching the heights of international acclaim, one of the most vital lessons I've learned is the importance of believing in one's own ability to adapt and thrive. Adaptability is not just beneficial in the dynamic world of publishing; it is essential. It means staying informed about industry shifts, being open to new writing and marketing methods, and exploring unfamiliar genres or formats. This adaptability goes hand in hand with continuous learning. Whether it's mastering your craft, understanding new technologies like AI, or navigating global marketing, there's always more to learn, and every new skill is a tool to help you thrive in a competitive market.

Another critical aspect of this journey is building resilience. The path of an author is inevitably marked by rejections, critiques, and setbacks. Developing the ability to bounce back from these challenges, viewing them as opportunities for growth rather than defeat, is crucial. However, as you adapt and learn, it's essential to stay true to your unique voice and vision. The authenticity of your perspective is what will make your work resonate with readers globally. Networking and collaboration are also key; building relationships with fellow authors, publishers, and industry professionals can open new opportunities and provide support and community.

Lastly, it's important to stay grounded. Success can be fleeting if not anchored in a clear sense of purpose. Remembering why you started writing in the first place should guide your decisions and path. In essence, the belief in your ability to adapt and thrive isn't just optimistic thinking; it's a mindset fostered through experiences, a commitment to growth, and an understanding of your strengths and values. It's this belief that will navigate you through the fluctuations of a writing career and lead you to your definition of success.

CHAPTER RECAP AND CONCLUSION

In this chapter, we embarked on a journey through the various stages of my writing career, from the humble beginnings of crafting a story for my daughter to achieving international acclaim. Each stage brought its unique challenges and rewards, offering valuable lessons that have shaped my journey as an author.

We started with the **Early Days**, where I emphasized the importance of embracing beginnings with optimism and creativity. This is where the seeds of a writing career are sown, and where the joy of creation should be your guiding force.

In **Scaling Up**, we looked at the transition from writing as a passion to recognizing its potential as a career. This phase is all about celebrating growth, embracing the surprises that come along the way, and learning to navigate the complexities of the publishing world.

International Acclaim highlighted the remarkable milestone of gaining global recognition. It's a testament to the power of storytelling and its ability to connect people across different cultures. This stage teaches us about the global impact of our work and the responsibility that comes with it.

The chapter concluded with **Key Lessons** about believing in your ability to adapt and thrive. Adaptability, continuous learning, resilience, and staying true to your unique voice are the cornerstones of a successful writing career. Building a network, staying grounded in your values, and always remembering why you started writing are crucial for long-term success.

As we close this chapter, remember that each writer's journey is unique. Your path may have different twists and turns, but the essence of the journey remains the same - a pursuit of creative fulfillment and professional growth. Embrace each stage with an open heart and mind, ready to learn, adapt, and thrive. The world of writing is vast and ever-evolving, and it awaits your unique contribution.

CHAPTER 2
UNDERSTANDING AI – A WRITER'S PRIMER

AI SIMPLIFIED - ENCOURAGEMENT TO FEARLESSLY EXPLORE NEW TECH

In the world of modern writing, embracing technology, particularly Artificial Intelligence (AI), is not just an option; it's a necessity for those looking to broaden their horizons and enhance their craft. As we venture into this chapter, our focus shifts to demystifying AI and empowering you to explore this revolutionary technology fearlessly.

AI can often seem daunting, shrouded in technical jargon and complex concepts. However, at its core, AI is simply a tool - a remarkably powerful one that can augment your creativity, streamline your writing processes, and open up new opportunities for you as an author. The key is to approach AI not as an insurmountable challenge, but as an exciting new palette for your creative expression.

This chapter aims to break down AI into understandable and relatable concepts. Think of AI as a partner in your writing journey, one that can take on various roles - from a meticulous editor who helps refine your prose to a market analyst providing insights into reader preferences. AI's versatility in the writing and publishing field is vast, and understanding this can transform the way you approach your work.

Embracing AI doesn't mean abandoning the traditional elements of writing that we hold dear. Instead, it's about enhancing those elements. It's about using AI to do more with your ideas, to reach deeper into your potential, and to connect with your readers in innovative ways. The goal is to show you how AI can be integrated seamlessly into your writing routine, making tasks easier and more efficient, allowing you more time to focus on the creative aspects of your work.

As we delve into the world of AI, I encourage you to keep an open mind. Let go of any apprehensions and embrace the curiosity that makes you a writer. Just as the pen and paper were once new tools for storytelling, AI is the new frontier. The potential for growth and exploration in this domain is limitless, and by the end of this chapter, you'll have a clearer understanding and hopefully, an ignited passion to fearlessly explore what AI can do for you.

AI IN WRITING: INSPIRING EXAMPLES TO OPEN YOUR MIND TO POSSIBILITIES

In the realm of writing, the integration of Artificial Intelligence (AI) is not a distant possibility, but a current reality that's reshaping the craft in exciting ways. The potential of AI in writing is vast and varied, offering authors a range of tools and applications that are transforming how they create, refine, and market their work. One inspiring aspect of AI in writing is content generation and enhancement. AI tools can generate creative content, provide story ideas, suggest plot developments, and even assist in enhancing narrative elements such as descriptions and dialogues, all while preserving the author's unique voice.

Another significant area where AI is making an impact is in editing and proofreading. AI-powered editing tools can meticulously analyze manuscripts for grammatical errors and stylistic inconsistencies, offering suggestions to improve readability and flow. These tools adapt to an author's style, making personalized recommendations that align with their unique voice. In understanding audiences, AI's role is indispensable. It can analyze reader data to provide insights on preferences and trends, helping authors tailor their work to better resonate with their target audience.

Moreover, AI is revolutionizing the marketing and distribution aspects of writing. It aids in creating targeted marketing campaigns, identifying optimal distribution channels, and even predicting market trends to position books more effectively. This includes optimizing social media strategies and email marketing campaigns. For authors aiming for international reach, AI-driven translation tools are invaluable, offering nuanced translations that maintain the original text's style and essence, thereby making works accessible to a global audience.

These examples illustrate just a fraction of AI's role in writing. AI's true value lies in its ability to be an asset in enhancing creativity, simplifying the writing process, and expanding an author's reach. As we delve deeper into the practical applications of these AI tools, authors are encouraged to view AI as a collaborator in their creative journey, one that introduces new dimensions to their craft and fosters deeper connections with their audience.

THE FUTURE OF AI: EXCITEMENT FOR WHAT THE FUTURE HOLDS FOR WRITERS

As we stand at the cusp of a new era in writing, the future of AI in this field is not only promising but also exhilarating. The advancements we're witnessing today are just the beginning, and the potential for AI to further revolutionize writing is boundless. For writers, this means entering a world where the creative process is augmented by technology in ways we are just beginning to imagine.

In the near future, AI is poised to become an even more integral part of the writing process. We can anticipate AI tools that offer more nuanced and sophisticated assistance in crafting narratives. These tools might be able to provide deeper insights into character development, plot structuring, and even thematic exploration, all aligned with the author's intent and style. Imagine an AI that doesn't just correct grammar but also suggests ways to enhance emotional impact or build suspense in a story.

Beyond the writing process, AI's role in personalized reader experiences is set to grow significantly. AI could enable writers to create more interactive and immersive stories, adapting in real-time to reader responses. This could herald a new form of storytelling where narratives are not just read but experienced, blurring the lines between books and interactive media.

In terms of market reach and understanding, future AI tools are expected to offer even more precise analytics, enabling writers to understand their audience like never before. This means being able to tailor stories to reader preferences, predict market trends, and effectively reach global audiences. The marketing of books could also see a transformation, with AI providing more innovative and effective ways to connect with readers and promote written work.

Moreover, AI's potential in bridging language barriers is vast. We might see highly sophisticated translation AI that not only translates text but also captures the nuances, humor, and cultural references, making stories universally relatable. This could open doors for authors to reach a truly global audience, breaking down the barriers that language often creates.

As exciting as these prospects are, it's important for writers to approach the future of AI with a blend of optimism and mindfulness. While AI will offer incredible tools and opportunities, the heart of writing will always remain human creativity and expression. AI is here to enhance, not replace, the human element of storytelling.

In conclusion, the future of AI in writing is a journey into uncharted territory, filled with possibilities that can elevate the art of storytelling to new heights. As authors, embracing these changes and learning to harness the power of AI will not only enhance our craft but also expand our reach and impact in the ever-evolving world of literature.

RECAP AND CONCLUSION

Throughout Chapter 2, we've explored the fascinating world of Artificial Intelligence (AI) and its transformative impact on the writing industry. We began by **simplifying AI**, breaking down its complex facade to reveal how accessible and beneficial it can be for writers of all genres and experience levels. This demystification was aimed at encouraging you to fearlessly explore and embrace new technological tools that can augment your writing process.

We delved into real-world examples of **AI in writing**, showcasing its applications in content generation, editing, audience analysis, marketing, and translation. These examples were designed to open your mind to the myriad possibilities AI offers, inspiring you to consider how these tools can enhance your creative expression and operational efficiency.

Looking ahead, we discussed the exciting **future of AI** in writing. The potential advancements in AI technology promise even more sophisticated assistance in narrative development, personalized reader experiences, precise market analytics, and advanced translation capabilities. This future is not just promising; it's thrilling for writers who are ready to embrace these changes and evolve with the times.

As we conclude this chapter, it's important to remember that AI is a tool meant to complement, not replace, the human element in writing. The essence of a great story lies in its ability to connect with readers on a human level, something that AI is designed to enhance, not supplant. As you move forward, I encourage you to view AI as a partner in your writing journey, one that offers new ways to express your creativity, reach a wider audience, and achieve greater success in your writing career.

CHAPTER 3
THE AUTHOR'S MINDSET FOR SUCCESS

GROWTH MINDSET: AFFIRMATIONS ON BLENDING CREATIVITY WITH BUSINESS SKILLS

IN TODAY'S LITERARY WORLD, WHERE CREATIVITY INTERSECTS with business acumen, it's crucial for authors to foster a growth mindset that embraces both aspects of their career. This mindset recognizes that creativity and business acumen are not mutually exclusive but rather complementary forces. As a writer, affirming your ability to blend these skills is key. Recognize that your creative talents breathe life into your stories, while your business skills ensure these stories find their audience and make an impact. Remind yourself that developing business savvy does not detract from your creativity; it's a tool that amplifies your voice and extends its reach.

Embrace the idea that learning in both writing and business is a continuous journey. Regularly affirm your openness to new knowledge and experiences, seeing each challenge as an opportunity to grow. This approach helps to overcome apprehensions, particularly about venturing into the less familiar business side of writing. Affirmations such as "I bravely embrace new challenges" or "I am equipped to handle the business aspects of my writing career" can instill confidence and resilience.

Setting achievable goals in both creative and business domains is vital, and celebrating every achievement, big or small, reinforces your growth. Maintaining a balance between creativity and practicality is essential. It's about allowing these two elements to coexist harmoniously, using affirmations like "I find a balance between my creative vision and practical business strategies" to keep them aligned.

Furthermore, acknowledge the importance of networking and collaboration. The writing journey is not a solitary path; it's enriched by interactions and partnerships that can expand both your creative and business perspectives. Affirmations like "I am open to collaborative opportunities that enhance my career" can lead to new and enriching experiences, contributing significantly to your growth as a modern writer.

By cultivating a growth mindset that values both creativity and business acumen, you empower yourself to navigate the multifaceted landscape of modern authorship. This balanced approach ensures that your stories not only captivate but also reach and resonate with readers worldwide.

OVERCOMING FEARS: REASSURANCE THAT CHALLENGES FUEL GROWTH

In the journey of any author, fears and challenges are inevitable companions. It's natural to encounter moments of doubt, especially when venturing into new territories like integrating AI into your writing or navigating the complexities of the publishing industry. However, it's essential to recognize that these challenges are not roadblocks, but catalysts for growth.

Embracing challenges as opportunities for development is a mindset shift that can have a profound impact on your career. Each obstacle faced and overcome is a step forward in your journey, building resilience, knowledge, and experience. Remember, the most successful authors are not those who never faced challenges, but those who faced them head-on and emerged stronger.

One common fear among writers, particularly when exploring new technologies like AI, is the worry of losing their creative essence. It's important to reassure yourself that tools and technologies are there to enhance your capabilities, not overshadow them. Affirmations like "I use challenges to fuel my growth and creativity" can be powerful in transforming apprehension into a positive driving force.

Another fear is the uncertainty of the market and how your work will be received. This uncertainty can be daunting, but it's also a reminder of the dynamic nature of the literary world. Each challenge in understanding and adapting to the market can teach you invaluable lessons about your audience, marketing strategies, and even your own writing.

In overcoming these fears, it's helpful to look back at your past achievements and challenges you've already surmounted. Reflect on how each experience has contributed to your growth as a writer. This reflection can provide the reassurance and motivation needed to tackle current and future challenges.

Also, don't hesitate to seek support when needed. Whether it's from fellow authors, mentors, or industry professionals, a supportive network can provide guidance, advice, and the reassurance you need to overcome challenges. Remember, asking for help is not a sign of weakness, but a step towards growth.

Embrace the challenges and fears that come your way, viewing them as opportunities to grow and enhance your craft. With each challenge you overcome, you not only become a more skilled and resilient writer but also open up new possibilities for your writing career. Let these challenges fuel your journey, pushing you towards new heights of success and fulfillment.

AI AS AN ALLY: POSITIVE OUTLOOK ON TECHNOLOGY ENHANCING WRITING

Embracing Artificial Intelligence (AI) in the realm of writing is not about yielding to a technological takeover; it's about recognizing AI as a valuable ally that can enhance and augment the creative process. This positive outlook towards AI is fundamental for authors who wish to stay relevant and competitive in a rapidly evolving literary landscape.

AI, when viewed as an ally, opens up a world of possibilities for writers. It's a tool that can take on the mundane, time-consuming tasks of editing and proofreading, allowing you more time to focus on the creative aspects of your work. AI-driven tools can offer suggestions that might spark new ideas or perspectives, enriching your storytelling. Imagine an AI assistant that helps you explore different plot scenarios, suggests character developments, or even provides feedback on narrative coherence and engagement.

Moreover, AI can be a powerful ally in understanding your audience. With advanced analytics, AI tools can provide insights into reader preferences and behaviors, enabling you to tailor your stories more effectively. This data-driven approach can lead to more engaging and relatable narratives, increasing reader satisfaction and broadening your fan base.

In marketing and distribution, AI's capabilities are equally beneficial. From optimizing your book's visibility in online marketplaces to identifying the most effective marketing channels and strategies, AI can significantly boost your book's reach and impact. It's about leveraging technology to ensure your stories find their way into the hands of eager readers.

It's important, however, to maintain a balance. While AI offers incredible tools and insights, the heart and soul of your story should always come from you, the author. AI is there to support and enhance your vision, not replace the unique voice and creativity that you bring to your writing.

In embracing AI as an ally, it's also crucial to stay updated with the latest developments in AI technology. This doesn't mean you need to become a tech expert, but having a basic understanding of the tools available and how they can benefit your writing process is essential.

Adopting a positive outlook on AI in writing opens the door to a host of benefits that can enhance your craft, streamline your processes, and expand your reach. By viewing AI as a collaborator, you can harness its power to enrich your storytelling, connect with your audience more effectively, and navigate the business aspects of your writing career with greater ease and success.

RECAP AND CONCLUSION

In this chapter, we have navigated the intricate relationship between an author's mindset and the successful integration of AI into their writing career. We began by emphasizing the importance of a **growth mindset**, highlighting how blending creativity with business skills is essential in today's literary world. Affirmations and a balanced approach between these two aspects help in fostering a mindset that is both creative and commercially savvy.

We then delved into **overcoming fears** and challenges, offering reassurance that these are not obstacles but rather stepping stones to growth and improvement. Embracing challenges with a positive mindset transforms them into opportunities for learning and development, which is crucial in the ever-evolving field of writing.

The chapter culminated with a discussion on **AI as an ally** in writing. We explored the positive outlook on how technology, specifically AI, can enhance and support the creative process. From taking over tedious tasks to providing valuable insights into reader preferences, AI emerges as a powerful tool that, when used effectively, can significantly augment an author's capabilities.

As we conclude this chapter, it's important to reflect on how these elements - a growth mindset, overcoming fears, and viewing AI as an ally - intertwine to create a robust framework for modern authors. Embracing these concepts opens up new avenues for personal and professional development, ensuring that you, as an author, are well-equipped to navigate the dynamic landscape of contemporary writing.

In your journey ahead, remember to keep these principles in mind. Cultivate a mindset that welcomes learning and growth, face challenges with resilience and optimism, and leverage AI as a tool to enhance your storytelling and reach. By doing so, you will not only enrich your writing experience but also expand your horizons in the ever-evolving world of literature.

CHAPTER 4
IDENTIFYING AI OPPORTUNITIES FOR AUTHORS

MARKET TRENDS: ENCOURAGE EXPLORATION OF NEW NICHES WITH AI INSIGHTS

In the rapidly evolving world of publishing, staying attuned to market trends is crucial for any author's success. AI offers unprecedented insights into these trends, enabling authors to identify and explore new niches that might have been previously overlooked. This section focuses on how AI can be used to encourage exploration of new niches and genres, potentially leading authors to untapped areas ripe for storytelling.

AI-driven market analysis tools are capable of sifting through vast amounts of data - from current bestsellers to reader reviews and online discussions. These tools can pinpoint emerging trends, shifts in reader preferences, and underrepresented genres in the market. By analyzing this data, authors can gain a clearer understanding of the literary landscape, identifying gaps that their writing could fill.

Exploring new niches with the help of AI doesn't just mean following the latest trends. It's about finding the intersection between your interests and unmet market demands. AI can help you explore genres or themes that align with your writing style while also having a potential audience waiting. This approach not only increases the chances of your work resonating with readers but also opens up new creative avenues for you as an author.

Furthermore, AI can track changes in reader sentiments and interests over time, providing a dynamic view of the market. This ongoing analysis can be invaluable for authors looking to evolve with their audience or those considering a pivot in their writing focus. It offers a strategic advantage in planning future projects or series.

However, while AI provides valuable insights, it's important to use this information judiciously. The goal is to inform and inspire your writing choices, not to dictate them. Balancing AI-driven insights with your unique creative voice is key. Let AI be a tool that broadens your horizons, not one that confines your creativity.

Leveraging AI to explore market trends and new niches can be a game-changer for authors. It opens up possibilities for innovation and differentiation in a crowded market. By harnessing the power of AI to understand and anticipate reader interests, you can strategically position your writing to capture the attention of new audiences, while continually refreshing and invigorating your creative journey.

SUCCESS STORIES: BE INSPIRED BY PEERS WHO'VE EMBRACED AI

In the journey of integrating AI into the writing process, there's nothing quite as inspiring as the success stories of fellow authors who have already embarked on this path. These stories not only demonstrate the practical benefits of using AI but also serve as a testament to the creative possibilities that this technology can unlock. In this section, we will explore several case studies of authors who have successfully harnessed the power of AI, providing tangible inspiration for those looking to follow in their footsteps.

Case Study 1: Tailoring Genres with AI Insights: One notable success story is of an author who used AI to analyze market trends and reader preferences, leading to a shift in genre focus. By leveraging AI-driven data, this author identified a growing interest in a particular sub-genre within fantasy. The decision to pivot to this sub-genre led to increased reader engagement and a significant boost in book sales, proving the value of AI in making informed strategic decisions.

Case Study 2: Enhancing Creativity with AI Assistance: Another inspiring example is an author who used AI tools for plot development and character creation.

The AI's suggestions were used as a springboard for creativity, leading to unique and compelling narrative arcs that the author hadn't initially considered. This collaboration with AI brought fresh perspectives to the author's work, resulting in a critically acclaimed novel that stood out for its originality.

Case Study 3: Streamlining the Writing Process: We also see success in authors who have utilized AI for editing and proofreading. One such author found that AI tools significantly reduced the time spent on editing, allowing for a quicker turnaround from manuscript completion to publication. This efficiency not only sped up the publication process but also allowed the author more time to dedicate to new writing projects.

Case Study 4: AI-Powered Marketing Strategies: Another area where authors have found success with AI is in marketing their books. One author used AI to analyze reader data across social media platforms, gaining insights into the most effective times and methods for promotion. By implementing an AI-driven marketing strategy, the author saw a marked increase in engagement and book sales.

These success stories are a powerful reminder of the multifaceted ways in which AI can be employed in the writing industry. From generating creative ideas to practical applications like market analysis and streamlined editing, AI is proving to be an invaluable asset for authors.

FUTURE OPPORTUNITIES: STAY CURIOUS AND OPEN TO EMERGING TRENDS

As the landscape of writing and publishing continues to evolve, staying attuned to emerging trends, especially those augmented by AI, is crucial for authors seeking sustained success. This section focuses on the importance of maintaining a sense of curiosity and openness to the ever-changing literary environment, ensuring that you are well-positioned to capitalize on future opportunities.

The world of AI in writing is rapidly advancing, and with it, new opportunities are constantly arising. Emerging trends might include AI-driven interactive storytelling, where readers become participants in the narrative, or advanced AI algorithms capable of generating sophisticated literary content that can inspire or complement your own creative ideas. The possibilities are as limitless as they are exciting.

To make the most of these opportunities, it is essential to cultivate a mindset of continuous learning and exploration. This involves keeping an eye on the latest technological advancements, staying informed about shifts in reader preferences and market dynamics, and being willing to experiment with new tools and techniques. Embrace AI not just as a tool for the present but as a gateway to future possibilities in the realm of writing.

Networking with other authors, attending industry

conferences, and participating in online forums can provide valuable insights into how AI is being used and the direction it is heading. These platforms offer a chance to learn from others' experiences, share knowledge, and stay connected with the pulse of the industry.

Furthermore, consider experimenting with emerging AI tools as they become available. While not every new technology will align perfectly with your needs or writing style, exploring these options can open doors to innovative approaches to storytelling, character development, or audience engagement that you may not have previously considered.

It's also important to keep an eye on how AI is influencing reader habits and preferences. The growing use of AI in recommendation systems, for instance, can affect how readers discover new books and authors. Understanding these trends can help you tailor your writing and marketing strategies to better reach and resonate with your audience.

The future of writing, interwoven with AI, is poised to bring forth exciting and innovative opportunities. By staying curious, open-minded, and proactive in exploring emerging trends, you can ensure that you are not just a spectator but an active participant in this evolving narrative. Embrace the journey ahead with enthusiasm and a willingness to evolve, and let your writing career be enriched by the endless possibilities that AI and future trends offer.

RECAP AND CONCLUSION

In this chapter, we've taken a deep dive into the dynamic world of AI in writing, exploring various facets that are shaping the future of authorship. We started by discussing the importance of staying abreast of **market trends**, highlighting how AI can provide valuable insights into reader preferences and emerging genres. By embracing AI in understanding these trends, authors can discover new niches and opportunities, potentially leading to untapped areas of storytelling.

We then looked at inspiring **success stories** of peers who have seamlessly integrated AI into their writing processes. These stories ranged from authors who used AI for enhancing creativity and narrative development to those who streamlined their editing processes and employed AI in effective marketing strategies. Each case study served as a testament to the diverse ways in which AI can contribute to an author's success.

Lastly, we focused on **future opportunities**, emphasizing the importance of maintaining a sense of curiosity and openness towards emerging AI trends in the literary world. The potential for AI to revolutionize writing is immense, and being prepared to adapt and experiment with new technologies is key to staying relevant and successful in this rapidly evolving field.

As we conclude this chapter, it's clear that the integration of AI in writing is not just a fleeting trend but a significant shift in the way we create and engage with literature. The intersection of AI and writing opens up a realm of possibilities that can enhance creativity, streamline processes, and connect authors with their readers in more meaningful ways.

Moving forward, I encourage you to view AI as a valuable tool in your writing arsenal, one that can help unlock new levels of creativity and efficiency. Stay informed, be open to experimenting with new technologies, and most importantly, continue to let your unique voice and storytelling prowess be the guiding force in your writing journey. The future of writing, enriched by AI, is an exciting one, and you have the opportunity to be at the forefront of this revolution.

CHAPTER 5
AI-DRIVEN STRATEGIES FOR AUTHORIAL EARNINGS

AI IN MARKETING: CONFIDENCE IN REACHING AND ENGAGING MORE READERS

IN THE DIGITAL ERA, THE MARKETING LANDSCAPE FOR authors has transformed dramatically, with AI playing a pivotal role in revolutionizing how books are promoted and readers are engaged. AI's ability to analyze extensive data sets equips authors with the tools for targeted audience reach, ensuring that marketing efforts are directed towards those most likely to be interested in their books. This level of precision not only increases the efficiency of marketing campaigns but also enhances the likelihood of connecting with the right audience.

Furthermore, AI enables the personalization of marketing content, tailoring messages to resonate with different segments of the audience. Whether it's through customized email campaigns or social media advertisements, AI's capacity to adapt content based on reader preferences and interests adds a personal touch to marketing efforts, significantly boosting reader engagement. The efficiency of AI in automating routine tasks, such as social media management and newsletter distribution, frees up valuable time for authors, allowing them to focus more on creative aspects of their marketing strategies or their writing.

Predictive analytics is another area where AI shines, offering insights that aid in strategic planning. By forecasting trends and predicting the effectiveness of various marketing channels, AI helps authors make informed decisions about where to invest their efforts and resources for maximum impact. Additionally, AI's role in enhancing social media engagement cannot be overstated. With tools to optimize post timings and analyze engagement patterns, AI aids in building a robust and interactive online presence, which is crucial for cultivating a community around an author's work.

The real-time feedback provided by AI on marketing campaign performance is invaluable. It allows authors to make quick adjustments, ensuring that their marketing strategies remain effective and relevant. This adaptability is key in a rapidly changing digital landscape, where staying ahead of trends and reader preferences is crucial for success.

In sum, AI has emerged as a formidable ally in the field of marketing for authors. Its capabilities in targeted audience reach, personalized content, efficiency, predictive analytics, and social media optimization empower authors to approach their marketing with a newfound confidence. By embracing AI's potential, authors can significantly enhance their visibility in the competitive marketplace and establish a deeper, more meaningful connection with their readership.

ENHANCING WRITING: OPTIMISM ABOUT AI ELEVATING YOUR CRAFT

The integration of Artificial Intelligence (AI) into the writing process opens up a world of possibilities for enhancing and elevating your craft. This section explores the optimistic outlook on how AI can be a valuable asset in your writing journey, offering new ways to enrich and refine your storytelling.

AI's role in enhancing writing begins with its ability to assist in the creative process. Tools like AI-driven writing assistants can offer suggestions for plot development, character arcs, and even dialogue refinement. These tools function by analyzing a vast array of literary works and writing styles, providing suggestions that can spark new ideas or help overcome writer's block. The key here is to view AI as a collaborative partner that augments your creativity, rather than as a replacement for your unique creative voice.

Beyond the initial creative phase, AI can significantly improve the editing process. AI-powered editing tools can analyze your work for grammatical errors, stylistic inconsistencies, and readability, offering suggestions that help polish your manuscript to a professional standard. This level of analysis, which can be both comprehensive and nuanced, often goes beyond what traditional editing software can offer, ensuring that your writing is not only error-free but also engaging and well-crafted.

AI can also play a role in enhancing the emotional impact of your writing. By analyzing the emotional tone and flow of your narrative, AI tools can suggest adjustments to ensure that your story resonates more deeply with readers. This can be particularly useful in genres where emotional engagement is key to the reader's experience.

In addition, AI-driven analytics can provide insights into how your writing is likely to be received by different audiences. By understanding reader preferences and trends, you can tailor your writing to appeal to specific reader groups, increasing the relevance and appeal of your work.

However, it's important to maintain a balance between leveraging AI and retaining your authentic voice. The aim of using AI in writing is to enhance and support your skills, not to overshadow the unique qualities that make your writing special. As you integrate AI into your writing process, let it inspire and assist you, but always keep your individuality at the forefront.

Adopting an optimistic outlook on the role of AI in writing can lead to significant enhancements in your craft. From aiding the creative process to refining the final manuscript, AI offers a range of tools that can elevate your storytelling. Embrace these tools with an open mind, and let AI be a catalyst for taking your writing to new heights of creativity and excellence.

DIVERSIFYING INCOME: EMPOWERMENT IN EXPLORING NEW REVENUE STREAMS

In today's diverse literary market, authors have the empowering opportunity to explore various revenue streams beyond traditional book sales, creating a more sustainable and robust financial base for their careers. The rise of audiobooks presents a lucrative avenue, allowing authors to tap into a growing audience that prefers audio formats. Digital platforms offer another realm of possibilities; subscription-based services like Patreon provide a platform for authors to offer exclusive content to subscribers, ranging from early access to works to special insights and bonus materials. Additionally, hosting writing workshops or webinars can harness an author's expertise for additional income.

Merchandising, based on themes or characters from books, opens up creative avenues for revenue. Collaborating with artists or designers to create unique merchandise can attract fans eager for a deeper connection with the story. Moreover, branching out into different writing formats or genres can diversify an author's portfolio, appealing to varied reader groups and expanding market reach.

For authors with a robust online presence, monetizing digital content through blog posts, videos, or social media can be fruitful. Advertising revenue and affiliate marketing are viable options for those who regularly produce engaging online content about writing, book reviews, or literary insights. Crowdfunding is another innovative approach, where platforms like Kickstarter can be used to fund unique book projects while simultaneously building interest and engaging with the reader community.

These diverse income streams not only provide financial stability for authors but also offer the freedom to explore creative projects without the sole reliance on traditional book sales. By embracing the myriad opportunities available in the digital age, authors can secure a more diverse and sustainable career, ensuring that their passion for writing is supported by a stable and varied income base.

RECAP AND CONCLUSION

Throughout this chapter, we've explored the transformative impact of Artificial Intelligence (AI) in various aspects of writing and authorship. We began by looking at how AI can significantly contribute to **marketing strategies**, offering authors confidence in reaching and engaging a broader audience. AI's ability to analyze and utilize large data sets helps in creating targeted and personalized marketing campaigns, ensuring that authors connect effectively with their readers.

We then delved into how AI can enhance the **writing process** itself. Far from replacing the writer's touch, AI acts as a valuable tool in augmenting creativity and refining the craft of writing. Whether it's through suggesting narrative improvements, aiding in character development, or providing sophisticated editing tools, AI is reshaping the way authors approach their work, infusing both efficiency and innovation.

The chapter also highlighted the importance of **diversifying income streams** for authors. In the evolving landscape of publishing and content creation, authors have numerous opportunities to explore beyond traditional book sales. From audiobooks and digital platforms to merchandising and collaborations, these alternate revenue streams not only ensure financial stability but also enable authors to connect with their audience in varied and creative ways.

As we conclude this chapter, it's clear that AI is not just a fleeting trend in the literary world; it's a significant force driving change and innovation. Its integration into various facets of writing and marketing represents a new era in authorship—one where technology enhances creativity and broadens possibilities. For authors willing to embrace these changes, AI presents opportunities to elevate their craft, reach wider audiences, and secure their financial footing in the industry.

In your journey as an author, keep an open mind

towards these evolving technologies and trends. Embrace the potential of AI to transform your writing and marketing strategies, explore diverse income streams, and stay attuned to the changing dynamics of the literary market. By doing so, you position yourself at the forefront of this exciting and dynamic era of authorship.

CHAPTER 6
PRACTICAL AI TOOLS FOR AUTHORS

TOOL SELECTION: ASSURANCE IN FINDING TOOLS THAT RESONATE WITH YOU

Navigating the expansive world of AI and technological tools available for authors today requires a strategic approach to ensure that you select tools that align with your unique writing and marketing needs. The key to successful tool selection lies in first understanding your specific requirements. Whether you need support in the creative process, assistance in editing and refining your work, or help with marketing and audience engagement, clearly identifying your needs will streamline your search for the right tools.

Once you've pinpointed your requirements, take advantage of trial periods and free versions offered by many AI tools. This approach allows for hands-on experimentation, giving you a sense of how well a tool integrates with your workflow and whether it complements your writing style. Additionally, recommendations from fellow authors and writing communities can be invaluable. Insights from peers who have firsthand experience with these tools can guide you towards options that have proven effective and user-friendly.

Ease of use and seamless integration with your current practices are crucial factors in tool selection. A tool should enhance, not complicate, your writing process, with a user-friendly interface and compatibility with other software or platforms you use. Customization and flexibility are also important; tools that allow for personalization to suit your specific projects or style can significantly improve their utility.

Moreover, cost-effectiveness is a vital consideration. While some tools offer advanced features, assess whether these align with the value they add to your work. Often, simpler and more affordable tools can meet your needs efficiently. Finally, consider the level of ongoing support and updates provided by the tool developers. Tools that are regularly updated and backed by responsive customer support are more likely to remain useful and relevant as your needs and the literary landscape evolve.

In summary, selecting the right AI tools for your writing and marketing efforts involves a careful balance of understanding your needs, experimenting with various options, seeking peer recommendations, and considering factors such as ease of use, customization, cost, and ongoing support. By taking these steps, you can find tools that resonate with your unique approach to writing, thereby enhancing your efficiency and creativity.

HANDS-ON TUTORIALS: ENCOURAGEMENT IN MASTERING NEW SKILLS

Embracing new technologies in your writing process often involves the challenge of mastering unfamiliar tools and features. To navigate this learning curve, hands-on tutorials play a crucial role. They provide step-by-step guidance, making the process of acquiring new skills more approachable and less daunting. Engaging with tutorials can significantly shorten the time it takes to become proficient with a new tool, whether it's an AI writing assistant, a marketing automation platform, or a data analytics program. These tutorials, often available online in various formats such as videos, webinars, or interactive modules, offer practical, real-world applications of the tools, enabling you to see immediate benefits in your work. They can also highlight lesser-known features or tips that can enhance your efficiency and creativity.

Encouragement in this learning process is key. Remember that mastering new technologies is an investment in your career as an author. Each new skill you acquire not only adds to your repertoire but also opens up new possibilities in how you approach your writing and marketing. It's important to be patient with yourself and recognize that proficiency comes with practice. Tutorials offer the support and guidance needed to build confidence in using these new tools, encouraging a mindset of continuous learning and adaptation. By dedicating time to these tutorials and embracing the learning process, you equip yourself with the skills needed to stay competitive and innovative in the ever-evolving world of writing.

BALANCING TECH AND TALENT: EMPHASIZING THE IRREPLACEABLE VALUE OF YOUR VOICE

In the midst of integrating advanced technologies like AI into your writing process, it's crucial to maintain a balance between technology and your inherent talent as a writer. This balance is key to ensuring that while you leverage the benefits of technology, the irreplaceable value of your unique voice and creative flair remains at the forefront of your work. Embracing AI and other digital tools should be seen as a means to enhance and complement your writing, not overshadow it. Your voice, with its distinct style, tone, and perspective, is what truly connects with readers and leaves a lasting impact.

It's important to remember that AI and technological tools are just that—tools. They are designed to assist, not replace, the creative intuition and emotional depth that you bring to your writing. While AI can suggest plot twists or correct grammatical errors, it cannot replicate the human experiences, emotions, and insights that you infuse into your stories. These human elements are what resonate with readers and make your work stand out.

Incorporating technology into your writing process requires a mindful approach. Use AI to streamline repetitive tasks or gain insights into reader preferences, but let the core of your writing—your ideas, experiences, and imagination—be guided by your talent. It's about finding the sweet spot where technology supports and amplifies your creative process without diluting the authenticity of your voice.

As you navigate this balance, it's also valuable to continuously hone your writing skills. Attend workshops, seek feedback, and engage with other writers to keep your talent sharp and in tune with your audience. This ongoing development of your craft ensures that your voice remains strong and clear, even as you adapt to new technologies.

The journey of integrating technology into your writing is not just about staying abreast with the latest tools but also about reinforcing the unique qualities that define you as a writer. By balancing tech and talent, you can harness the full potential of AI and digital tools to enhance your writing, while ensuring that the essence of what makes your work uniquely yours—your voice—continues to shine through.

RECAP AND CONCLUSION

In this chapter, we've explored the multifaceted role of AI and technology in enhancing the modern author's journey. We began by addressing the importance of **selecting the right tools**, emphasizing that finding technologies that resonate with your specific needs and style is crucial. This process involves understanding your requirements, experimenting with different tools, and seeking recommendations to ensure you choose tools that enhance, rather than complicate, your writing process.

We then discussed the value of **hands-on tutorials,** which play a vital role in helping you master new skills associated with these technologies. These tutorials not only make learning more manageable but also ensure that you can quickly integrate new tools into your workflow, enhancing both efficiency and creativity.

A significant focus of the chapter was on **maintaining a balance** between technology and your inherent talent. While AI and digital tools offer numerous advantages, they should serve as aids to your creativity, not replacements. Your unique voice and creative flair are irreplaceable, and preserving this authenticity is key. Technology should amplify your talent, not overshadow it.

It's clear that the intersection of technology and writing is rich with opportunities for growth and innovation. However, the heart of your writing — your unique voice and perspective — remains the most critical element. In your journey forward, embrace these technological tools, but always let your individuality lead the way. By striking this balance, you can utilize AI and technology to their fullest potential, enhancing your writing and reaching new heights in your authorship.

CHAPTER 7
ETHICAL WRITING IN THE AGE OF AI

AI ETHICS: CONFIDENCE IN NAVIGATING NEW ETHICAL LANDSCAPES

In the realm of AI and writing, navigating the ethical landscape is as crucial as mastering the technology itself. As AI becomes increasingly integrated into the creative process, authors must be cognizant of the ethical implications and maintain a responsible approach. This section delves into the importance of understanding and confidently navigating the new ethical landscapes that emerge with the use of AI in writing.

One of the primary ethical considerations is the authenticity and originality of the work. While AI can assist in generating content and ideas, it's vital to ensure that the final output is distinctly your own, maintaining the integrity of your voice and creativity. Authors should use AI tools as catalysts for inspiration, not as crutches for creation, ensuring that their work remains an authentic expression of their ideas and experiences.

Another key aspect is data privacy and consent, especially when using AI tools that analyze reader data to gain insights into preferences and trends. It's important to adhere to data protection laws and respect the privacy of your audience. Transparency with readers about how their data is being used and ensuring it is handled ethically builds trust and upholds your reputation as an author.

AI also raises questions about the potential for bias in content creation. AI algorithms are often trained on existing data, which can reflect historical biases. Authors need to be aware of these potential biases and actively work to ensure their use of AI doesn't perpetuate stereotypes or exclude certain groups. This awareness involves critically evaluating the outputs of AI tools and making conscious efforts to represent diverse perspectives in your work.

In addition, there are considerations around the intellectual property of AI-generated content. Authors should be informed about the legal aspects of using AI-generated content and ensure that their use of such content does not infringe on the rights of others. Understanding the legalities surrounding AI-assisted work is essential to avoid potential disputes and uphold ethical standards.

As AI continues to reshape the landscape of writing, it brings with it a new set of ethical considerations. Navigating these effectively requires a combination of awareness, responsibility, and a commitment to upholding ethical standards. By understanding and addressing these ethical dimensions, you can confidently integrate AI into your writing practice, ensuring that your work not only benefits from technological advancements but also adheres to the highest ethical standards.

DATA PRIVACY: EMPOWERMENT IN PROTECTING AND RESPECTING DATA

In the age of digital technology and AI, data privacy has become a paramount concern, particularly for authors who increasingly rely on digital tools and platforms. Understanding and respecting data privacy not only protects your work and your readers but also empowers you as an author to operate with integrity and trust. This section focuses on the significance of data privacy in the writing process and how authors can navigate this crucial aspect with confidence.

The empowerment in protecting and respecting data starts with a thorough understanding of the types of data you might encounter or collect, such as reader demographics, preferences, and feedback. It's essential to be aware of the laws and regulations regarding data privacy, such as the General Data Protection Regulation (GDPR) in the European Union or other local data protection laws. These regulations outline your responsibilities in handling personal data and provide guidelines to ensure that this data is collected, processed, and stored securely.

As an author, you should be transparent with your readers about the data you collect and how it will be used. Clear communication about your data practices builds trust and demonstrates your commitment to respecting your audience's privacy. This could involve providing privacy notices or consent forms, especially when collecting data for marketing purposes or personalized content.

Implementing robust security measures is also a key aspect of data privacy. This includes using secure platforms and tools for data collection and storage, as well as adopting practices like regular data audits and secure password protocols. Being proactive in protecting the data you handle not only safeguards your readers' privacy but also protects your reputation as an author.

Moreover, being selective about the data you collect is important. Collect only the data that is necessary for your intended purpose, and avoid unnecessary data accumulation. This practice, known as data minimization, reduces the risk of data breaches and helps maintain a focus on data that is truly valuable for your writing and marketing efforts.

Embracing the responsibility of data privacy is crucial in today's digital and AI-driven writing landscape. By understanding the legal requirements, being transparent with your readers, implementing strong security measures, and practicing data minimization, you empower yourself as an author who respects and protects personal data. This approach not only fosters trust among your readers but also ensures that you navigate the digital realm with ethical integrity and confidence.

RESPONSIBLE AI USAGE: POSITIVITY ABOUT SETTING ETHICAL AI STANDARDS

In the evolving landscape of writing enhanced by AI, setting and adhering to ethical AI standards is not just a responsibility but also a positive step towards sustainable and respectful technology use. This section emphasizes the importance of responsible AI usage and the benefits of maintaining high ethical standards in its application.

Responsible AI usage begins with a thorough understanding of how AI tools function, the principles behind their algorithms, and the implications of their use. It's crucial for authors to be aware of the origins of the data used by these AI tools and the potential biases they may carry. By being informed, authors can make conscious choices about the AI tools they use, ensuring that these tools align with their ethical standards and the expectations of their readers.

Positivity in setting ethical AI standards also involves actively seeking out AI tools and platforms that prioritize ethical practices. This includes tools that are transparent about their data sources, algorithms, and functionalities. By choosing AI partners that adhere to ethical guidelines, authors can ensure that their use of AI is responsible and aligned with their values.

Moreover, authors have the opportunity to be advocates for ethical AI usage in the writing community. Sharing knowledge about ethical AI practices, discussing the implications of AI in writing forums, and participating in dialogues about the future of AI in literature can help raise awareness and set a standard for responsible usage. This proactive approach not only benefits the individual author but also contributes to a broader culture of ethical AI use in the literary world.

It's also beneficial to continuously review and update your understanding of AI ethics, as this is a rapidly evolving field. Staying informed about the latest developments, challenges, and discussions in AI ethics ensures that your practices remain current and responsible.

Embracing responsible AI usage and setting high ethical standards is a positive and necessary approach in today's technology-driven writing environment. By being informed, choosing ethical AI tools, advocating for responsible practices, and staying updated on AI ethics, authors can lead the way in ensuring that AI is used in a way that respects both the art of writing and the rights of individuals. This responsible approach not only aligns with ethical principles but also enriches the writing process, fostering a harmonious relationship between technology and creativity.

RECAP AND CONCLUSION

In this chapter, we have delved into the critical aspects of ethical considerations surrounding the use of Artificial Intelligence (AI) in writing. We began by exploring the importance of **AI ethics**, emphasizing the need for authors to confidently navigate new ethical landscapes that emerge with AI integration. Understanding and adhering to ethical guidelines ensures that the use of AI in writing is responsible and respectful of both the craft and the audience.

We then addressed the crucial topic of **data privacy**, underscoring the empowerment that comes with protecting and respecting the data involved in our writing processes. By being informed about data protection laws, being transparent with our audience, and implementing robust security measures, we maintain the trust of our readers and uphold our integrity as authors.

The chapter concluded with a focus on **responsible AI usage**, highlighting the positive impact of setting and following high ethical standards in AI application. This responsibility extends beyond personal practices to advocating for ethical AI usage within the wider writing community. By staying informed and actively participating in discussions about AI ethics, authors can contribute to a culture of responsible AI use in literature.

It's clear that ethical considerations are integral to the successful and respectful use of AI in writing. Whether it's navigating the ethical implications of AI-generated content, ensuring data privacy, or advocating for responsible AI usage, these considerations are crucial for authors in the digital age. By embracing these ethical principles, we not only enrich our own writing practices but also contribute positively to the evolving narrative of AI in the literary world. Moving forward, let us carry the mantle of ethical responsibility, ensuring that our use of AI in writing is as principled as it is innovative, and as respectful as it is transformative.

CHAPTER 8
OVERCOMING WRITING AND AI CHALLENGES

TECHNICAL CHALLENGES: MOTIVATION TO TACKLE AND MASTER NEW TECHNOLOGIES

In the journey of integrating AI and new technologies into the writing process, authors inevitably face technical challenges. These challenges, however, should not be seen as obstacles but as opportunities for growth and skill development. This section is dedicated to providing motivation and guidance for tackling and mastering these new technologies, enabling you to fully harness their potential in enhancing your writing career.

The first step in overcoming technical challenges is adopting a mindset that views each challenge as a learning opportunity. Whether it's understanding complex AI algorithms, navigating new software interfaces, or keeping up with the latest digital tools, approach these tasks with curiosity and determination. Remember, every technical skill you acquire not only improves your writing process but also adds to your versatility and value as an author.

It's important to set realistic goals and timelines for mastering new technologies. Breaking down the learning process into manageable steps can make it less daunting and more achievable. Start with the basics before moving on to more advanced features. Celebrate small victories along the way, as each step forward is progress.

Seeking resources and support can significantly ease the learning curve. Many AI tools and digital platforms offer tutorials, user guides, and customer support. Additionally, online courses, webinars, and writer forums can be invaluable sources of information and advice. Don't hesitate to reach out to fellow authors or tech-savvy professionals for tips and insights.

Practicing patience and persistence is key. Becoming proficient with new technologies takes time, and there may be setbacks along the way. Maintain a positive attitude and keep pushing forward, understanding that each challenge you overcome enhances your capability to utilize these technologies effectively.

Finally, integrate what you learn into your regular writing routine. The more you use these technologies in your day-to-day activities, the more comfortable and skilled you will become in handling them. This hands-on experience is crucial in moving from understanding to mastery.

Technical challenges in adopting new technologies are an inevitable part of an author's growth in the digital age. By approaching these challenges with a positive mindset, setting achievable goals, utilizing available resources, practicing patience, and integrating new skills into your daily routine, you can turn these challenges into opportunities to enhance your writing and expand your capabilities. Embrace the journey of mastering new technologies, and let it propel your writing to new heights of innovation and efficiency.

CREATIVE CHALLENGES: ENCOURAGEMENT TO KEEP CREATIVITY FLOWING WITH AI

In the rapidly evolving landscape of AI-enhanced writing, authors may encounter creative challenges as they integrate these new technologies into their craft. However, these challenges should be viewed not as hindrances but as opportunities to invigorate and expand one's creative horizons. This section aims to provide encouragement and strategies for maintaining a steady flow of creativity while leveraging the capabilities of AI.

One of the key aspects of overcoming creative challenges with AI is maintaining an open mindset. AI can offer unexpected insights and suggestions that might diverge from your initial ideas. Embrace these moments as opportunities to explore new creative pathways. The unique input from AI can lead to fresh perspectives and ideas that you might not have considered otherwise.

It's also important to find the right balance between AI assistance and your creative intuition. While AI can provide valuable data and suggestions, the essence of your story should always stem from your imagination and narrative voice. Use AI as a tool to enhance your storytelling, not dictate it. Let AI spark ideas, but allow your creativity to drive the narrative.

Experimentation is another key to keeping your creativity flowing with AI. Try out different AI tools and features to see how they can best serve your writing process. This could involve using AI for character development, plot suggestions, or even to overcome writer's block. Each experiment can open up new ways of thinking about and approaching your stories.

Remember, too, that creativity is not always a linear process. There will be times of abundant ideas and times when inspiration seems scarce. During these ebbs and flows, be patient with yourself and the process. AI can be a valuable ally in these periods, providing a nudge to your creativity when needed.

Lastly, don't hesitate to step away from technology when necessary. Sometimes, the best way to recharge your creativity is to disconnect from all tools and immerse yourself in the world around you. Inspiration can come from the simplest of experiences, and taking a break from technology can provide a fresh perspective.

While AI introduces new dynamics to the writing process, it also brings exciting opportunities to enhance and challenge your creativity. By embracing an open mindset, finding the right balance, experimenting, being patient, and occasionally stepping away from technology, you can effectively use AI to enrich your creative journey. Let AI be a companion that inspires and complements your storytelling, pushing your creative boundaries to new heights.

STAYING AHEAD: ENTHUSIASM FOR BEING A PART OF AI ADVANCEMENTS

In the fast-paced world of AI and its applications in writing, staying ahead involves not just keeping up with current advancements but also embracing them with enthusiasm. This section is dedicated to fostering an excitement for being an active part of the AI revolution in writing, encouraging authors to see these advancements as opportunities to grow, innovate, and redefine the boundaries of storytelling.

Staying ahead in the realm of AI requires a proactive approach. This means regularly updating your knowledge about the latest AI developments and understanding how they can impact and enhance your writing. Follow tech blogs, subscribe to industry newsletters, and participate in relevant webinars and workshops. This continuous learning not only keeps you informed but also fuels your enthusiasm for the potential of these technologies.

Engaging with the AI writing community is another

crucial aspect. Connect with other authors who are using AI in their work, join online forums, and participate in discussions about AI in writing. These interactions provide valuable insights into how others are leveraging AI, offering inspiration and new ideas for your own work.

Experimentation is key to staying ahead. Be open to trying out new AI tools and features as they emerge. Even if not all new technologies fit your current needs or style, the act of experimenting itself can be enlightening and invigorating. It keeps your approach to writing fresh and adaptable to changing technologies.

Moreover, approach AI advancements with an open mind and creative spirit. Consider how each new development in AI can open doors to unexplored narrative techniques, storytelling formats, or character development processes. AI advancements are not just tools for efficiency but catalysts for creative exploration.

Finally, share your experiences and learnings with the wider community. Whether it's through blog posts, social media, or speaking engagements, contributing your insights on AI in writing helps build a collective understanding and enthusiasm for these advancements. Sharing also reinforces your own learning and positions you as an active participant in the AI writing community.

Embracing AI advancements with enthusiasm and a proactive mindset is essential for authors looking to stay ahead in the rapidly evolving landscape of writing technology. By continuously learning, engaging with the community, experimenting, and sharing your experiences, you become not just a witness to this revolution but an active and influential part of it. Let your enthusiasm for AI advancements drive your journey into new realms of creativity and innovation in writing.

RECAP AND CONCLUSION

In this chapter, we've delved into the various dimensions of integrating AI into the writing process, addressing the challenges and opportunities it presents. We started by exploring the **technical challenges** that come with adopting new technologies, offering motivation and strategies to tackle and master them. Emphasizing that these challenges are not roadblocks but learning opportunities, we discussed the importance of a step-by-step approach, utilizing resources, and maintaining patience and persistence.

We then shifted our focus to the **creative challenges** that AI integration can pose. Encouragement was provided to maintain and fuel creativity, suggesting a balanced approach where AI acts as a tool to inspire and enhance rather than dictate the creative process. Experimentation with AI was highlighted as a key method for finding new avenues of creative expression.

The chapter concluded with a discussion on the importance of **staying ahead** of AI advancements in the writing field. We emphasized the value of proactively engaging with ongoing developments, maintaining enthusiasm for new possibilities, and participating actively in the AI writing community. This engagement not only keeps your skills and knowledge current but also positions you as a key player in the evolving narrative of AI and writing.

As we wrap up this chapter, it's clear that the journey of integrating AI into writing is multifaceted, involving continuous learning and adaptation. Whether it's overcoming technical hurdles, keeping the creative juices flowing, or staying abreast of the latest advancements, each aspect contributes to a richer, more efficient, and more innovative writing process. Embracing AI in writing is not just about keeping up with the times; it's about actively shaping and enhancing your craft. As you move forward, carry with you the lessons learned, the creativity sparked, and the enthusiasm for what lies ahead in the ever-evolving world of AI-enhanced writing.

CHAPTER 9
THE COMPLETE AI AUTHOR'S TOOLKIT

ESSENTIAL SKILLS: POSITIVITY ABOUT EXPANDING YOUR SKILL SET

IN THE CONSTANTLY EVOLVING LANDSCAPE OF WRITING AND publishing, especially with the integration of AI and digital tools, authors must continually expand their skill set. This expansion is not just a necessity but an exciting opportunity for growth and innovation. This section focuses on fostering a positive outlook towards developing essential new skills that can enhance your writing career.

Embracing the acquisition of new skills with positivity is crucial. The learning process can be challenging, but approaching it with enthusiasm transforms it into an enriching experience. Skills such as mastering new writing software, understanding AI algorithms, learning about digital marketing, or even delving into data analysis can significantly enhance your capabilities as an author.

Consider the broad spectrum of skills that contemporary authors need. Beyond writing, these include digital literacy, understanding online reader engagement, data-driven decision-making, and effective use of social media for promotion. Developing these skills not only enhances your ability to reach and connect with audiences but also empowers you to take control of various aspects of your writing career.

Continuous learning and skill development also keep your approach to writing dynamic and adaptable. The publishing world is rapidly changing, and staying updated with relevant skills ensures that you remain competitive and relevant. Engaging in regular training, whether through online courses, workshops, or self-study, keeps your knowledge base fresh and your approach innovative.

Moreover, expanding your skill set opens up new avenues for creativity and exploration. For instance, understanding the nuances of AI can lead to new ways of storytelling or character development. Skills in digital marketing can open doors to broader and more diverse audiences. Each new skill adds another dimension to your craft.

Remember, the journey of learning is ongoing and iterative. Each new skill builds upon the last, creating a rich tapestry of knowledge and experience that enhances every aspect of your writing. Celebrate each milestone in your learning journey, and view each challenge as an opportunity to grow.

Adopting a positive attitude towards expanding your skill set is essential for any author navigating the modern literary landscape. By continually learning and embracing new skills, you not only enhance your writing and marketing capabilities but also open yourself to new possibilities and experiences in your writing career. Let this journey of skill expansion be a source of inspiration, driving you towards greater success and fulfillment in your craft.

NETWORKING: ENCOURAGEMENT TO BUILD SUPPORTIVE, INNOVATIVE COMMUNITIES

In the dynamic world of writing and publishing, the importance of networking cannot be overstated. Building a network of supportive, like-minded individuals and communities is not just beneficial for professional growth, but it also fosters a culture of innovation and collaboration. This section emphasizes the value of networking and offers encouragement to authors to actively seek and nurture these connections.

Networking in the writing community can take many forms, from joining local writer's groups and attending literary events to participating in online forums and social media platforms. These interactions provide opportunities to share experiences, gain insights, and offer mutual support. Engaging with a diverse range of authors, editors, publishers, and marketers can expose you to different perspectives and ideas, enriching your own understanding of the industry.

Building a network also opens doors to collaborative opportunities, which can be invaluable in expanding your reach and exploring new creative avenues. Collaborations can range from co-authoring projects to shared marketing efforts, each bringing together different strengths and audiences for mutual benefit.

Moreover, a supportive community can be a source of motivation and inspiration, especially during challenging times. The writing journey is often solitary, but having a network means you're not alone in facing the obstacles and uncertainties that come with a writing career. Whether it's advice on navigating the publishing landscape or feedback on a manuscript, a strong network can provide the support and encouragement needed to persevere and succeed.

In the context of AI and digital advancements in writing, networking becomes even more crucial. Staying connected with fellow authors who are also exploring these new tools and technologies can lead to shared learning and innovation. Discussions within these networks can provide insights into how best to integrate AI into your writing, the ethical implications to consider, and the latest trends to watch out for.

Actively building and participating in writing communities is a crucial aspect of a successful writing career. It offers not just professional advantages but also emotional and creative support. Embrace the process of networking with enthusiasm and openness, recognizing that each connection made is a step towards building a more supportive, innovative, and collaborative writing environment. Let these connections inspire and propel you forward in your journey as an author.

LIFELONG LEARNING: INSPIRATION TO CONTINUALLY EVOLVE WITH AI

In the ever-changing landscape of writing, where AI and digital technologies continually reshape the way stories are told and shared, adopting a philosophy of lifelong learning is crucial. This commitment to ongoing education and adaptation is not just a necessity for keeping pace with technological advancements but also a source of inspiration and personal growth. In this section, we explore the importance of lifelong learning in the context of evolving with AI in the writing industry.

Embracing lifelong learning means staying curious and open to new ideas, techniques, and technologies that emerge in the realm of AI and writing. It involves regularly updating your knowledge and skills, whether through formal education, online courses, workshops, or self-directed study. This continuous pursuit of knowledge keeps your writing fresh and relevant, ensuring that you are always at the forefront of technological and creative trends.

The rapid development of AI technologies offers a particularly rich field for lifelong learning. As AI tools become more sophisticated, they open up new possibilities for storytelling, character development, and reader engagement. Keeping abreast of these advancements allows you to incorporate the latest tools into your work, enhancing your storytelling capabilities and connecting with audiences in innovative ways.

Moreover, lifelong learning in the context of AI is not just about mastering new tools and technologies. It's also about understanding the broader implications of AI in literature, including ethical considerations, the impact on reader engagement, and the changing dynamics of the publishing industry. This broader understanding informs your use of AI, ensuring that it aligns with your creative vision and ethical standards.

The journey of lifelong learning is also a journey of personal transformation. Each new skill acquired and concept understood contributes to your development as a writer and as an individual. It fosters a mindset of adaptability and resilience, qualities that are invaluable in the fast-paced world of modern writing.

Lifelong learning is an essential component of evolving with AI in the writing industry. It offers a pathway to continually refresh and expand your skills, stay relevant in a rapidly changing field, and draw inspiration from new technological and creative frontiers. Embrace this journey with enthusiasm and an open mind, and let it guide you to new heights in your writing career.

RECAP AND CONCLUSION

In this chapter, we delved into the essential components of the AI Author's Toolkit, focusing on the key areas that modern authors need to embrace for success in an AI-driven literary landscape. We began by emphasizing the importance of expanding your **skill set**. Recognizing that the writing world is constantly evolving, especially with AI advancements, we discussed the need to continually acquire new skills. This pursuit not only keeps you competitive but also opens up new creative possibilities, enhancing both the quality and reach of your work.

Next, we turned our attention to the power of **networking**. Building a network of supportive, like-minded individuals is invaluable in today's interconnected writing community. Whether it's through online forums, writer's groups, or literary events, connecting with other writers and industry professionals provides a wealth of resources, opportunities for collaboration, and a sense of community. These connections are essential for sharing knowledge, finding inspiration, and navigating the ever-changing landscape of AI in writing.

Lastly, the chapter highlighted the importance of **life-long learning** in the context of AI. Keeping pace with the rapid advancements in AI technology requires an ongoing commitment to learning. This continuous education is not just about staying relevant; it's about embracing the exciting new opportunities that AI offers for storytelling, reader engagement, and more efficient writing processes. Lifelong learning ensures that you are always at the cutting edge, ready to utilize the full potential of AI in your writing.

As we close this chapter, it's clear that the AI Author's Toolkit is multifaceted, encompassing skill development, networking, and lifelong learning. Each of these components plays a crucial role in ensuring that you are well-equipped to thrive in the AI-enhanced world of writing. By embracing these elements, you prepare yourself not just to adapt to the changes brought by AI but to actively leverage them to your advantage, enhancing your creativity, efficiency, and connectivity in the writing community.

CHAPTER 10
CRAFTING YOUR AI-ENHANCED WRITING STRATEGY

PERSONALIZED STRATEGY: CONFIDENCE IN CREATING A PATH THAT SUITS YOU

In the diverse and ever-evolving world of AI-enhanced writing, there is no one-size-fits-all strategy. The key to successfully integrating AI into your writing process lies in developing a personalized strategy that aligns with your individual style, goals, and needs. This section is dedicated to fostering confidence in creating a path that uniquely suits you as an author.

Developing a personalized strategy starts with a deep understanding of your own writing process. Reflect on the stages of your writing where AI could be most beneficial. Are you looking to streamline the research process, enhance creativity in storytelling, or perhaps improve efficiency in editing? Identifying specific areas for AI integration ensures that the tools and techniques you adopt are directly relevant to your needs.

It's also essential to consider your comfort level with technology. While some authors may be eager to dive into the most advanced AI tools available, others might prefer a more gradual approach, starting with simpler, more intuitive technologies. Choose tools that match your tech-savviness and willingness to learn, ensuring that the integration of AI into your writing process is enjoyable rather than overwhelming.

In formulating your strategy, set clear and achievable goals. Whether it's improving the quality of your writing, increasing productivity, or expanding your audience reach, having specific objectives helps guide your decisions on which AI tools and techniques to adopt. Regularly assess the effectiveness of these tools in meeting your goals, and be prepared to adjust your strategy as needed.

Remember, your personalized strategy should also evolve over time. As you become more comfortable with existing AI tools, explore additional or more advanced options that could further enhance your writing. Stay informed about new developments in AI and be open to experimenting with emerging technologies.

Most importantly, trust in your unique voice and perspective as an author. AI is a powerful tool, but it's your creativity and storytelling that drive your writing. Your personalized strategy should amplify these elements, not overshadow them.

Having confidence in creating a personalized AI strategy is a crucial aspect of embracing technology in your writing. By understanding your needs, setting appropriate goals, choosing the right tools, and staying open to growth and adaptation, you can develop a strategy that not only enhances your writing process but also aligns with your individuality as an author.

MEASURING SUCCESS: CELEBRATION OF EVERY MILESTONE ACHIEVED

In the journey of integrating AI into your writing process, measuring success is not just about the end result, but also about recognizing and celebrating every milestone along the way. This section focuses on the importance of acknowledging your progress, big or small, and how it contributes to a sense of accomplishment and motivation in your writing journey.

Success in utilizing AI can take various forms and it's important to set both short-term and long-term goals to gauge your progress. Short-term goals might include successfully integrating an AI tool into your daily writing routine, or completing a piece of writing using AI-assisted research. Long-term goals could be broader, such as improving the overall quality of your writing, achieving higher efficiency, or gaining a larger readership. Each goal achieved, regardless of its scale, is a step forward in your journey and deserves recognition.

Celebrating these milestones is crucial. It not only provides a sense of achievement but also boosts your confidence and enthusiasm to tackle further challenges. Acknowledging your progress reinforces the positive impact that AI is having on your writing process and motivates you to continue exploring and integrating these technologies.

Moreover, measuring success should also include reflecting on the learning process itself. Every challenge overcome and every new skill acquired in the process of adopting AI is a success in its own right. These achievements contribute significantly to your growth as a modern author, equipped to navigate the evolving landscape of writing and publishing.

It's also beneficial to share your successes with your network. Whether it's a small win or a major milestone, sharing your journey can inspire others and provide opportunities for mutual learning. This shared celebration fosters a supportive community among fellow authors and those interested in AI-assisted writing.

Measuring success in the realm of AI and writing is about more than just the final outcomes. It's about celebrating every milestone, learning from each step, and acknowledging your growth along the way. By taking the time to recognize and celebrate these achievements, you maintain a positive and motivated outlook, paving the way for continued success and innovation in your writing career.

STAYING FLEXIBLE: OPTIMISM IN ADAPTING TO AND EMBRACING CHANGE

In the ever-evolving landscape of AI in writing, one of the most critical attributes for authors is the ability to stay flexible. Embracing change and adapting to new tools and methods are essential for thriving in this dynamic environment. This section emphasizes the importance of maintaining an optimistic outlook as you navigate these changes, viewing each new development as an opportunity for growth and improvement in your craft.

Staying flexible means being open to experimenting with different AI tools and techniques, even those that may initially seem outside your comfort zone. The world of AI is vast and varied, offering a plethora of options that can enhance various aspects of writing and publishing. By exploring these options, you open yourself up to discovering tools that could significantly streamline your writing process, open new creative avenues, or help you connect with your audience more effectively.

An optimistic approach to adapting to change also involves viewing setbacks and challenges as learning experiences. The integration of AI into writing is not always a smooth journey; there will be moments of frustration or confusion. However, each of these challenges is an opportunity to learn more about the capabilities and limitations of AI, and how best to apply it to your work.

Flexibility also extends to how you perceive the role of AI in writing. It's important to remember that AI is a tool to assist and enhance your abilities, not replace them. As AI technology continues to advance, staying adaptable allows you to find the right balance between utilizing AI and retaining the human touch that is central to creative writing.

Furthermore, being flexible means keeping an eye on the future and being prepared to continuously evolve your approach to writing. The field of AI is rapidly advancing, and what is cutting-edge today may become outdated tomorrow. Staying informed about the latest developments and being ready to integrate new advancements into your writing ensures that you remain at the forefront of this exciting field.

Staying flexible and optimistic in the face of change is a vital aspect of incorporating AI into your writing. By embracing new technologies, viewing challenges as opportunities for growth, and being prepared to continuously adapt, you set yourself up for ongoing success and innovation in your writing career. Let your adaptability be the key that unlocks the full potential of AI in enhancing your craft.

RECAP AND CONCLUSION

This chapter has taken us on a journey through the critical steps of developing a **personalized strategy** for integrating AI into the writing process. We started by emphasizing the importance of creating a path that suits your individual needs and preferences. Recognizing that each author's approach to writing is unique, we discussed how to choose AI tools and techniques that align with your specific style and goals, ensuring a harmonious integration of technology into your creative process.

We then moved on to the significance of **measuring success**. Celebrating every milestone in your journey with AI is crucial, as it not only marks your progress but also boosts your confidence and motivation. Whether it's mastering a new AI tool, enhancing a particular aspect of your writing, or achieving a broader reach with your audience, each achievement is a step forward in your AI-enhanced writing journey.

Finally, the chapter highlighted the importance of **staying flexible** and optimistic in the face of change. Adapting to new technologies and methods is a continuous process, and maintaining a positive outlook is essential for embracing these changes. Flexibility in your approach allows you to effectively incorporate AI advancements, ensuring that your writing stays relevant and innovative.

As we conclude this chapter, it's evident that crafting an AI-enhanced writing strategy is a dynamic and ongoing process. It involves a thoughtful selection of tools, a celebration of progress, and an adaptable mindset to the ever-changing technological landscape. By embracing these elements, you pave the way for a future in writing that is not only technologically advanced but also creatively fulfilling. Let this journey be one of discovery, growth, and continual evolution, as you harness the power of AI to elevate your writing to new heights.

EPILOGUE
WRITING INTO THE FUTURE

EMBRACING CHANGE: EXCITEMENT FOR THE EVOLVING ROLE OF AI IN WRITING

Embracing the evolving role of AI in writing is a journey filled with both excitement and discovery. As AI continues to reshape the landscape of storytelling, it offers writers the chance to explore new dimensions of creativity and efficiency. This section delves into the enthusiasm surrounding these changes and the potential that AI holds for enhancing the art of writing.

The evolution of AI in the literary world is not just about the advancement of technology; it's about the new doors it opens for writers. AI offers tools for deeper character development, more intricate plot structures, and even suggestions for stylistic enhancements. These tools don't limit creativity; instead, they provide a springboard for writers to leap from, enabling them to reach heights that might have seemed unattainable before.

There's a certain thrill in experimenting with AI-driven tools. Whether it's using AI to generate initial ideas or employing sophisticated software for editing and refining your work, each interaction with AI can lead to unexpected and inspiring results. This process of exploration and experimentation is invigorating, pushing writers to think outside the box and approach their craft from new angles.

Furthermore, AI's capabilities in understanding and predicting reader preferences can be a boon for writers. By providing insights into what readers enjoy, AI can help tailor stories to resonate more deeply with the audience. This not only enhances the reader's experience but also increases the writer's ability to connect with their audience on a more profound level.

However, embracing the evolving role of AI in writing also means being aware of and adapting to its challenges. As AI tools become more integrated into the writing process, maintaining the balance between human creativity and technological assistance is crucial. The goal is to use AI as a complement to your skills, ensuring that your unique voice remains the driving force behind your stories.

The growing role of AI in writing is a source of excitement and potential for writers. It invites a reimagining of traditional writing processes and opens up a world of new possibilities. By embracing these changes with an open mind and a sense of adventure, writers can use AI not only to enhance their craft but also to redefine the boundaries of storytelling.

CALL TO ACTION: A RALLYING CRY TO BE PIONEERS IN AI INTEGRATION

As we stand at the forefront of a new era in writing, where AI and technology are rapidly transforming the landscape, there is a compelling call to action for authors: to be pioneers in AI integration. This rallying cry is not just about adopting new tools; it's about leading the charge in exploring how AI can redefine storytelling, enhance creativity, and open up unprecedented possibilities in the literary world.

Being a pioneer in AI integration means venturing into uncharted territory with a spirit of exploration and innovation. It's about being willing to experiment with AI tools, to learn and adapt, and to share your experiences with the wider writing community. You have the opportunity to set examples, to blaze trails, and to shape the future of how AI is used in writing.

This call to action is also an invitation to contribute to the ongoing dialogue about the role of AI in literature. It's about engaging in discussions, offering insights, and raising important questions regarding the ethical implications, the balance between human creativity and AI, and the future direction of AI in writing. Your voice and perspective as an author are invaluable in shaping these conversations.

Moreover, being a pioneer means embracing AI with a mindset of collaboration. AI is a partner in your creative process, offering new ways to approach your craft. By harnessing the power of AI, you can push the boundaries of your storytelling, explore new narrative techniques, and connect with your readers in innovative ways.

However, pioneering is not without its challenges. It requires resilience, adaptability, and a continuous commitment to learning. The landscape of AI is ever-evolving, and staying informed and agile is key to navigating its changes successfully.

The call to action is clear: step forward as pioneers in the integration of AI into writing. This is your moment to lead, explore, and influence the future of storytelling. Embrace AI not just as a tool, but as a catalyst for innovation and creativity. Let your journey with AI be a testament to the endless possibilities that technology and human creativity can achieve together.

FINAL THOUGHTS: VISION OF A FUTURE WHERE AI AND CREATIVITY COEXIST

As we close this exploration into the integration of AI in writing, we look forward to a future where AI and creativity coexist harmoniously, each enhancing the other. This vision of the future is not one where human creativity is overshadowed by technology, but rather where AI acts as a catalyst, unlocking new levels of expression and storytelling.

In this future, AI tools are seen as partners in the creative process, offering insights and assistance that amplify the writer's inherent talents. Imagine AI not just as a technical aid but as a source of inspiration, a collaborator that brings a new dimension to the art of storytelling. This collaboration enables writers to delve deeper into their imagination, explore uncharted narrative territories, and connect with their audience in more meaningful ways.

This vision also sees a writing community that is more connected and empowered. With AI breaking down barriers, writers have access to a global audience and a wealth of resources that were previously unimaginable. This interconnectedness fosters a richer, more diverse literary landscape, where ideas and stories from different cultures and perspectives are shared and celebrated.

Moreover, the future of AI in writing is one of ethical responsibility and thoughtful integration. As AI continues to evolve, so too does our understanding of its impact. Writers play a crucial role in shaping how AI is used, ensuring that it upholds the values of authenticity, diversity, and ethical practice. This conscious integration of AI paves the way for a future where technology enhances human creativity while respecting the core principles of storytelling.

The journey of integrating AI into writing is just beginning, and the possibilities are as boundless as our imagination. As authors, embracing AI with an open mind and a creative spirit allows us to be at the forefront of this exciting evolution. Let us move forward with a vision of a future where AI and creativity coexist, each enriching the other, as we continue to tell stories that captivate, inspire, and connect us all.

FAQS
REASSURANCE IN ANSWERING COMMON CONCERNS AND QUERIES

Q1: Will AI replace human writers?
A: No, AI is not designed to replace human writers. Its purpose is to assist and enhance the writing process. AI can provide tools for idea generation, language improvement, and editing, but it cannot replicate the unique creativity, emotion, and personal experience that human writers bring to their work.

Q2: How can I ensure that my work remains original when using AI?
A: To ensure originality, use AI as a support tool rather than a source. Let AI provide suggestions and ideas, but make the final decisions yourself. Your personal insights, experiences, and creative choices are what will keep your work original and authentic.

Q3: Is it difficult to learn how to use AI writing tools?
A: The difficulty can vary depending on the tool, but many AI writing tools are user-friendly and designed with the writer's needs in mind. Most come with tutorials, customer support, and user guides to help you learn. As with any new tool, there's a learning curve, but with practice, it becomes more manageable.

Q4: Can AI help me become a better writer?
A: Yes, AI can contribute to improving your writing skills. AI tools can offer suggestions on grammar, style, and structure, which can help you learn and grow as a writer. They can also assist in research and provide data-driven insights into writing effectively for your target audience.

Q5: How can I stay updated with the latest AI tools and technologies in writing?
A: Stay updated by following tech blogs, subscribing to industry newsletters, joining writing and tech forums, and participating in webinars or workshops focused on AI in writing. Networking with other writers and tech enthusiasts can also provide valuable insights into the latest trends.

Q6: Will using AI limit my creative freedom?
A: Not at all. In fact, AI can enhance your creative freedom by taking care of routine tasks and offering novel suggestions, allowing you more space and time to focus on the creative aspects of your writing.

Q7: How can AI influence my writing style?
A: AI can offer suggestions that might refine or enhance your writing style, but it doesn't dictate it. You maintain control over your narrative voice and style. AI tools can help identify areas for improvement or suggest alternative phrasing, but these are just options for you to consider. Ultimately, your writing style remains uniquely yours.

Q8: Is AI writing technology expensive?
A: The cost of AI writing tools varies. There are many affordable, even free, options available that offer basic features. More advanced tools with sophisticated capabilities might come with a subscription fee. It's about finding a tool that fits both your needs and your budget.

Q9: Can AI help with writer's block?
A: Yes, AI can be a valuable tool in overcoming writer's block. AI-powered idea generators, content suggesters, and even AI-driven research tools can provide inspiration and new perspectives when you're stuck.

Q10: How does AI handle different genres of writing?
A: Many AI writing tools are designed to be adaptable to various genres. They can analyze and make suggestions based on the nuances and stylistic elements typical of different genres, from fiction to technical writing. However, it's always important to use your judgment and ensure the AI's suggestions fit the context of your specific genre.

Q11: What if the AI makes suggestions that don't fit my vision?

A: It's perfectly fine to reject AI suggestions that don't align with your vision. The goal of using AI is to aid your creative process, not to override your creative choices. Use AI as a tool for ideas and suggestions, but trust your instincts as a writer.

Q12: How can I ensure ethical use of AI in my writing?

A: Ethical use of AI involves being transparent about how much of your work is AI-assisted, ensuring the originality of your content, and being mindful of privacy and data protection laws if your AI tools process reader data. It's also about being aware of potential biases in AI tools and striving to avoid perpetuating them in your writing.

JAMIE CULICAN
AUTHOR, MARKETER, PUBLISHER, TEACHER

Jamie is a USA Today bestselling author with a passion for helping other authors succeed. She is the owner of Dragon Realm Press, a publishing house that specializes in working with indie authors. With over a decade of experience in the publishing industry, Jamie has become an expert in book marketing, book design, and book editing. Her approach is centered on creating a personalized and collaborative experience for her clients that results in high-quality, marketable books.

Her extensive marketing background allows her to guide authors through the complex world of book promotion, providing them with strategies that work. Jamie believes that every author has a unique voice, and she is committed to helping them share their stories with the world.

With a focus on innovation, Jamie has been at the forefront of integrating AI into the publishing industry. She believes that AI is a powerful tool that can help authors streamline their processes and reach new audiences. Jamie is passionate about helping authors navigate the ever-changing landscape of publishing and achieve their goals.

linkedin.com/in/jamie-culican

MELLE MELKUMIAN
AUTHOR, TECHNOLOGIST, MARKETER, PUBLISHER

Melle has spent her career translating complex technology for the lay person, working with prestigious organizations such as NASA, Northrop Grumman, and Hewlett Packard. As the Marketing Director for an AI-enabled app company, Melle continues to leverage technology to drive meaningful change. She believes we are at a pivotal moment in history, where the incredible potential of AI is set to revolutionize the way we work and live. Melle is passionate about helping people navigate this shift and harness the power of AI to achieve their goals. Her expertise and unique perspective make her an invaluable resource for anyone looking to tap into the full potential of AI in their personal or professional life.

Outside of her professional career, Melle is a USA Today bestselling author, having published multiple books with rave reviews through a fresh approach to fantasy storytelling. Through her work as an author, Melle has gained a deep understanding of the writing and publishing process, and how emerging technologies like AI can support and enhance the creative process. She is excited to share her expertise and insights with fellow authors in the AI for Authors community.

linkedin.com/in/melleamade

AI4CES
EMPOWERING PROFESSIONALS, TRANSFORMING INDUSTRIES

AI4CES, the AI-focused educational platform designed to empower individuals across a wide range of vertical markets, including publishing, proposal and grant writing, and education. With our mission to make AI accessible to everyone, we provide comprehensive, tailored learning experiences through online classes, webinars, and more. Our expertly crafted courses break down complex AI concepts into digestible, easy-to-understand lessons, enabling you to harness the power of AI and revolutionize the way you work in your industry.

Don't miss the opportunity to stay ahead in today's competitive landscape by mastering AI with AI4CES. Our adaptive, engaging, and interactive learning modules ensure that you receive personalized, cutting-edge education in a format that suits your needs and preferences. Join the AI revolution with AI4CES and transform the way you approach challenges in your profession, from publishing to grant writing and beyond.

www.AI4CES.com

facebook.com/ai4ces
linkedin.com/company/ai4ces

www.ingramcontent.com/pod-product-compliance
Lightning Source LLC
Chambersburg PA
CBHW070424240526
45472CB00020B/1187